This boo

If found

mithmoth.com

Made in the USA
Las Vegas, NV
12 September 2023

77468517R00072